The Love Birds

Tom Poole

The Love Birds

Copyright © 2024 by Thomas P. Poole

First paperback edition April 2024

Book design by Katherine LE White

ISBN 9798884960299

After their wedding, Uncle Willie and Aunt Rose thanked everyone for coming and cut the cake they bought at the A and P. They hugged everyone good night then Willie and Rose set out to drive to Asheboro. They were going to spend the honeymoon night at the Carolina Motel. Willie reached over and playfully placed his right arm around her right shoulder and pulled her to him. He softly touched her.

"Willie, since we are married, you can go farther now."

He drove all the way to Greensboro.

Aunt Rose and Uncle Willie were sitting on their front porch when a fella drove up and called to Uncle Willie.

"How do you get to Rockingham?"

"My nephew usually takes me." Willie nodded and smiled.

When Whit Miller walked out of the post office in Candor, he saw Uncle Willie sitting in his old Plymouth with Joe Dog sitting at the steering wheel.

"Ole Joe Dog do most of your driving?"

"Not since he wrecked my pickup truck," Willie said.

A policeman stopped Uncle Willie for driving too slow and blocking the highway. He sternly glared at Uncle Willie. "I'm giving you a ticket," the gruff policeman said.

"Oh, good. When are they going to hold the drawing?" Uncle Willie was not a winner.

U ncle Willie and Aunt Rose were walking on one of those tourist paths up in the Smoky Mountains when suddenly a bear jumped out from behind a tree. It reared up on its hind feet and let go with a loud horrible growl.

Aunt Rose grabbed Willie's arm and said, "Do something."

He said, "I just did."

Matt Hurley asked Aunt Rose how Uncle Willie was doing. She said he was doing real fine and staying home to play checkers with old Joe Dog. Matt thought she was teasing, so he asked her again. "Can Joe Dog really play checkers?"

"Oh yes," she said, "Willie taught him how to play last winter."

"Can Joe Dog play pretty good?"

"Not really. Willie can beat him three out of five games."

A woman walked up to Uncle Willie at the Piggly-Wiggly when he was working part time and asked him if they had French Dip.

"No ma'am, all we have is a bladder of Railroad Sweet. Not many women dip snuff now these days."

Little Willie was asked one day where his heart was. He smiled, stood up at his desk, and patted the back of his pants.

The teacher said, "No, Little Willie, your heart is in the middle of your chest." She pointed to his chest.

"No, it is back there. I know that because when Grandma comes to see us on Sunday, she hugs me and pats me on the backside and says, bless your little heart."

Uncle Willie's feet are so big that he has to pull his pants on over his head to get them on.

Aunt Rose was telling her next-door neighbor the latest news. "Willie was held up by two men last night."

Clarissa gasped, "For Heaven's sakes, where?"

"All the way home."

U ncle Willie went to the Fire Station to check out the new fire truck. There were six or seven men kicking the tires, rubbing the siren, and admiring the red paint. Woodrow Hinson, the fire chief, was in Fireman's Heaven with all the praise he got for getting the new firetruck.

Uncle Willie stepped forward and asked the fire chief what they would do with the old fire truck.

Woodrow strutted across the firehouse, snapping his red suspenders and knocking the cap off of a Coca Cola bottle. "Well, boys, I have thought about that a lot. I finally figured out what to do with it."

All the men stopped talking and looked Woodrow in the face.

"I have decided to keep the old firetruck and use it for false alarms."

U ncle Willie and six men belonging to the Highway 27 Hunting Club somehow managed to get a hunting license in Florida. The license was for two alligators. After a good bit of getting ready for the trip, only four men could make it. Willie and Dallas Green rented a boat, loaded their high-powered guns and pushed off in search of alligators. Dennis Green and Jason Jordon did the same and the four alligator killers were on the hunt.

About two hours before sunset, the horror of all horrors took place. A ten-foot-long alligator came up from the side of Willie and Dallas' boat and bit Dallas' right leg off. After the panic and shooting into pinecones, Dallas was taken to a hospital. Willie called Dallas' home and told his wife that an alligator had bitten off one of his legs off.

Dallas' wife was in shock. "Which one?"

"I don't know. All them alligators look alike to me."

Saturday morning, Uncle Willie and Aunt Rose went over to Little River fishing. There at the ford, Uncle Willie crossed over and walked upstream as she walked upstream. As the river widened, Uncle Willie started yelling across to Aunt Rose.

"What are you trying to say?" she asked.

"I said, I'm trying to figure out how to get on the other side of the river."

"You are on the other side of the river."

He looked around and never said another word.

U ncle Willie stopped by the Pure Station and asked Raymond Dunn if he would go to Troy with him. Raymond jumped in the passenger seat and the two were off.

"What are we going to Troy for?" Raymond inquired.

"I seen the Thompson brothers yesterday. Steve said he went to Troy and got a New Jeep for his wife, Molly. I figured I would go over there and see what I can get for Rose."

Uncle Willie said he smelled smoke coming from under the wood stove in the front room. He ran to the telephone and called the Fire Station.

"Help, help!" Willie shouted into the phone. "The house is on fire!" Then he hung up.

The fire department said that they had to wait until the morning to find out whose house had burned down.

Aunt Rose called the firehouse and told them that Uncle Willie had just fell in the well. "They needed to come right over," she said.

The fire chief, Woodrow Hinson, asked her if she knew how deep he was.

She said he was up to his knees.

The Fire Chief said they would hurry over to rescue Willie. They would not have to turn the siren on or call an ambulance.

Rose called out, "Oh yes, you will. Willie fell in head first!"

W illie took his mule to the sale in Asheboro. It was a big thing; horses, mules, hogs, goats, and sheep, any kind of stockyard animal. When he got there, one of the workers noticed that Willie's mule was sick. The man told Willie to take his mule away and do not bring it back.

Willie went back to Candor and decided to raffle the mule off. It was a winner. At a dollar a ticket, Willie would make a lot of money. He was going to make a very good profit. Tuesday night was the drawing for the mule and everything seemed to be doing okay. Wednesday morning, the poor old mule was dead.

The local vet came over to take a look at the mule, making sure nothing was contagious. He looked Willie eye to eye and said, "I heard you raffled off a dying mule. I bet a lot of people are mad at you."

Willie laughed, "Nobody got mad at me. Jack Jackson was the winner, and I gave him his dollar back."

Willie went over to Doris Meachum's house to plant 200 tulips she bought in Southern Pines. She saw him at the Tractor Place just out of Candor and he agreed to plant the tulips for her. She was a tight old woman and tried to get the cheapest man to work for her. He set to work around nine in the morning and finished at five in the evening. He was proud of his work.

Doris offered him no water, no lunch and kept peeping out the window to make sure he was working. When she saw him stop work, she came out with a smile on her face. "It is lovely Willie, just lovely." He cleared his throat and smiled at her. "When they come up, Willie, I will pay you."

Willie grabbed the shovel and started digging the tulips. "Well, Mrs. Meachum, go get your pocket-book, they is coming up now."

U ncle Willie heard that a Taco Bell was coming to town.

"What do we need another telephone company for?"

Willie said that Leroy Timken was so cheap that he went bald so he would not have to pay for haircuts and hair products.

Uncle Willie and Aunt Rose took a neighbor to the funeral home. Her husband had passed away and they were helping her as she took care of all the things a widow has to do. Sally was very old and her children had drifted off to other places. Some might be able to make the funeral and a couple just could not make it. After choosing the casket and the tombstone, Sally was relieved to find out about her husband's funeral, because he served in the Army during the war. She finished the obituary and groaned as she eased out of her chair.

The undertaker explained, "The obituary has to be so many words and you have four more words. What would you want to add?"

Sally said, with a weary sigh, "Pickup truck for sale."

Chapter 22

Uncle Willie was so knock-kneed and Aunt Rose was so bow-legged, when they stood together, they spelled out OX. Willie always said Rose was too bowlegged, she could not hem a hog in a fence. Willie Jr. says that OX meant love and kisses.

Uncle Willie said that when Willie Jr. was a baby, he was so bowlegged that if you threw him, he would come back just like a boomerang.

Uncle Willie and several men were standing at the main corner in Candor when a funeral procession passed by. They all doffed their hats and stood respectful as the procession slowly passed.

"Who died?" one of the men asked Uncle Willie.

"The fellow in the first car," Willie said.

Little Willie went running into the living room where Big Willie was watching television.

"Pop, come quick! A wild cat done jumped in the window where mama is sewing."

"It'll be alright son, if he got in by himself, he can get out himself."

A loving couple like Uncle Willie and Aunt Rose have times when they have a spat. Most of the time, everything is wonderful. A few months ago, there was a little spat that both lovers did not see coming.

One morning at breakfast, Willie told Rose that he was getting tired, not as happy as he had been. In fact, he was thinking pretty hard about living.

Rose said that she agreed that she had noticed things were not as they had been. Then she told Willie to hold up a few minutes, she would get her hat and pocketbook and go with him.

A unt Rose said that Willie and she had moved. She was calling the family and telling them where they would be moving.

"Why?" was the one question that people asked.

"Well, Willie read in the Greensboro Morning Paper that most accidents occur within twenty-five miles of home. So, he moved closer to Norman and farther from home. The address will be the same, though, because Willie took the mailbox with us."

Aunt Rose asked Willie to sit down and talk about serious family business. She told him that they were not getting along, and people were noticing it. She was ashamed to face her friends, and she felt that Willie was the same way. No one in either family had ever divorced.

"That would shame both sides of the family, but little Willie would be hurt worse than us. So, I sat down last night and prayed to the Lord. I want the Lord to take one of us and I will go live with my sister."

Uncle Willie was doing some yard work for Doris Meachum and had to get a truckload of cow manure. He loaded the bed of the truck at the nursery. The truck was overloaded, causing the front end to lift so that the truck was hard to steer and hard to drive. Willie normally drove slow, but with the difficulty of this load he drove really slow. In fact, there was a line of about twenty cars long behind him.

A highway patrolman (formally a state trooper) met Willie in that long curve and turned around and stopped Willie. He was one of those patrolmen that walked with that puckered butt strut. In his most sarcastic manner snapped at Willie, "Have you got governors on this truck?"

Uncle Willie looked up with a smile, "No sir, I ain't. That is cow manure you smell. The Governor is in Raleigh."

Ollie Wilson stepped inside the café and glanced around the six customers at the counter. He walked over to Uncle Willie. "My goodness, you ain't dressed for Leroy Timken's funeral, ain't you going?'

"Naw, I think I will skip it."

"Him and you was good friends, I can't believe you ain't going. Not even to the viewing last night?"

"Why should I? He ain't going to mine."

Willie was widely known for his cheapness. Leroy Timken said he thought the cheapest thing Willie ever did was when Willie Junior paid for a trip to Disneyworld and bought airplane tickets for Willie and Rose.

When they got off the plane at Greensboro on the return trip, Aunt Rose said, "Thank goodness we had a safe flight."

"We wasted five-dollars on flight insurance," Willie said.

Uncle Willie and Silas Bogsford were helping build a storage shed for Charles Bogsford Grocery Store. Willie shuffled off towards the outhouse. About 15 minutes later, Willie opened the door to the outhouse and stuck his head out and called Silas.

"What do you need Willie? You need some paper?"

"Find me a long limb or a tobacco stick. I dropped my coat down the hole."

"You ain't going to wear that nasty thing are you?"

"Of course not, but my lunch is in my coat pocket."

Uncle Willie and Naylor Nelms were discussing the changes in the world. They'd come to the conclusion that the morals were collapsing.

"I did not sleep with my wife until we got married. What about you?" Naylor asked Willie.

"What was her maiden name?" Willie said.

U ncle Willie went to fill out papers for his social security.

The lady asked him what his birthday was.

He said November 5th.

She said, "What year?"

"Why every year," was his answer.

At Christmas, Uncle Willie was working part time at the Piggy-Wiggly for a little extra money. He was working the turkey freezer. The turkeys were all stacked up and shoppers dug through them trying to find the turkeys they needed for their table. A woman ran up after she went through the freezer and asked Willie if the turkeys got bigger.

He said, "No ma'am, them turkeys is all dead. They cannot get bigger."

The lady looked at him like he was crazy. Both of them walked off thinking they had met the dumbest person that they had ever met.

Cecil Hurley came across Uncle Willie and Paul Dunn dragging a big buck deer out the woods. They could not lift the buck up, much less carry him. They settled for dragging him by his hind legs and having a devil of a time doing it. The antlers were catching on every little tree and snag.

Cecil said, "Why don't you boys drag him by the antlers? It would be a lot easier."

After taking his advice, a half hour later Willie turned and said to Paul, "Ole Cecil was right about how easy it would be to drag it by the antlers."

"Yeah," Paul agreed, "it makes it easy, but we are getting too far from the truck."

U ncle Willie built a wood stove out of 2x4s. Don't laugh, it worked once.

There was a large crowd around Uncle Willie's watching his house burn. Spud Carson walked up to Willie and was trying to console him. "I'm sorry about your house burning, Willie."

"That's alright, Spud, I have enough wood in the attic to build another house."

A friend stopped by Uncle Willie's house last Friday. He was delighted. The other day he finally got around to taking his spring bath and he found two sets of long underwear he did not know that he had.

The horn blew in Willie's front yard. It was his buddies picking him up for his Monday Night Hunt Club meeting. Out of respect, two of the members sat in the back seat and allowed Willie to sit on the passenger's side so he could see the road. Carl Privett was the driver.

"I see you need curtains for your bedroom," one of the men in the back said. There was a giggle and a hiccup at the end of his question.

"That is Rose's job. She usually makes them herself," Willie said.

"Oh, she needs to make them now," the other backseat passenger said. It was followed by another giggle and another a silly giggle.

"What in the world are you talking about?" Willie put in.

"Ah, Willie I stopped by Saturday night to see if you wanted to go out for a couple of beers. When I cut off my head-lights, I saw you and Rose playing a game of slap and tickle. I was a little embarrassed and thought I would start up and sneak off to keep you two being bothered. You certainly need to get curtains fixed." Carl said. The two in the backseat broke up with laughter.

"Well, the joke is on you. Me and Leroy went off to Capelsie and fished from sunset to sunrise. I wasn't even there Saturday."

Not another word was spoken. The two men in the back seat got quiet.

L eroy Timken said that Willie wasn't even fit to help make up a crowd.

S everal of the local men were sitting around the Pure Oil Station Saturday morning. They had solved the state problems and were getting ready to solve the national problems. Leroy Timken drew out his pocket watch, wound it up and slipped it back into his pocket.

"Hmmmmm," he said, "it is twelve o'clock. I thought it was later than that."

"It don't get no later than twelve o'clock. After twelve o'clock it starts all over again," Willie said.

Larry Miller had a nice lot on Lake Tillery. He kept it in good repair and when something else caught his eye he would install it. He had two boats, one was a pontoon and the other was a restored 1940 inboard. His favorite was a canoe. When he felt like the world was crashing in on him, he pulled the canoe out and went up the Uwharrie River and paddled away. His wife enjoyed the house, the flowers, the evening walks up the dirt road that ran alongside the Pee Dee River. She always sang Swanee River when she took her evening walk. Stephen Foster had picked the Pee Dee River for his song but wound up using Swanee River. When Larry went up the Uwharrie, she would wave and let him go.

U ncle Willie and Aunt Rose had been given invitations for Sarah Hall and Charles Honeycutt's wedding. That was a big party. Over one hundred people, counting family, showed up. Uncle Willie saw Larry Miller push his canoe into the river and load it up for an all- day adventure.

Willie ran over to Larry and handed him a quart of the best white lightning in Montgomery County. "Take this with you. If you are low, a couple of swallows will have you smiling before you get a half mile away."

"Thank you, Willie. I needed this." Larry opened the lid and lifted the jar for a long drink. He screwed the lid tightly on and set the jar beside him. He took his paddle and began his journey. Willie turned and staggered towards the party.

L arry did not like to see a lot of people when he was in his melancholy state of mind. He liked to paddle along and just feel the sun or the rain on his face and arms. Jack London could have not asked for more. Larry paddled fast and hard. On and on into the heart of the river when the bodies of deer floated along and in the summer rattlesnakes paid too much interest in humans.

When the sun began to set, Larry turned to go home. Odd, he thought, he had paddled his canoe hundreds of times, but this time, something was different. He felt lost. Nothing seemed to be in the right place. There should be people cooking out and children playing along the river banks. He paddled faster, and ever faster. He just could not understand what was happening. Finally, he stopped to get his bearings. He slowly looked for a land marker or another boater. When he looked left and then down at the river, he suddenly realized he had been tied up all day on his pier.

"Lordy," he said, "that is some of the best white lightning I have ever tasted in my life.

It was preaching all day and dinner on the church grounds. There were nine tables and each table was filled with some of the best cooking the South ever had. The preacher stepped out to let another preacher give him a rest. The preacher had filled the largest plate at the table and stacked the plate with six persimmon puddings. He walked up to Aunt Rose and Uncle Willie with a smile on his face.

"Miss Rose, isn't this just wonderful?"

"Oh yes. I could not eat another bite."

"I've had about a belly full myself," Uncle Willie added.

Leon Timken stopped by Uncle Willie's house to make sure he was doing well. He had given him and Aunt Rose a very nice bathroom set with six different brushes. For some reason, Leon thought it was the perfect Christmas gift.

"Willie, how do you like the toilet brush set?"

"Rose really likes it, but I would rather use toilet paper."

Willie read in the Greensboro paper that married men live a lot longer than single men. The way he saw it, that if you wanted to die a slow death get married.

Willie called the fire department one night. "Help, help, my barn is on fire."

"How do we get there?" asked the man on the other end of the line.

"Ain't you still got that red fire truck?"

"I mean how do we get to your house?" the man said with a heavier voice.

"I'm south of Candor on old Highway 220. It'll be the only house with the barn on fire."

Uncle Willie went up to the tobacco grower's office and said his tobacco crop was in bad shape. He was told that his tobacco was really a fungus with black rot. Not sure what all that was, he wrote Raleigh and asked for help. About a week later several cars pulled up in his yard. All those cars had about four people in them. All the cars had a big North Carolina seal on the door and hood. Several men got out and went straight to the tobacco field. One man was the leader and he went right up to Willie and said "That is the worst black root rot I have ever seen."

"I'm sorry, but it is the best I have," Willie meekly said.

Around October some of the local farmers met at the Tractor Repair. The summer had been hot and suddenly the rain was a major problem. Everything was soaking wet to the wet fields of the fall planting to the hog pens. The cost of feeding the hogs was the main topic. It looked like a few farmers had taken a loss. Willie was really upset. He listened to one of those radios that can be heard all the way from Nebraska and Idaho. "Out there the hogs are bringing in a lot more money.", he said. He wanted to drive out there to sell his hogs.

Joe Thompson told Willie that would not work. "It is very far away, the gasoline would cost a lot. And just think of the time involved."

Willie thought for a few minutes and then said, "What's time to a hog?"

Willie was drinking coffee at the M and R Café with the boys. The subject chosen by Willie was the difference in churches and especially how weddings were conducted. He had been to a wedding last Saturday afternoon that he had not heard before. Usually, the preachers ask them to say I Do. The church that is used as a service station on Sunday uses something different and the bride's husband-to-be answers the question.

Lonnie Hall leaned over to Willie and asked him what the man said. Willie said,"Don't shoot."

Willie was sitting in the barber shop talking with the unofficial town council. Doc, the barber and the town intellectual, read aloud from the morning paper.

"It says that tomatoes are high in cholesterol."

"Yeah, they're high right here in Candor too," Willie put in.

When Willie and Rose heard the news that the Walk on Water quartet was coming to Charlotte to give a concert at the Charlotte Coliseum, they immediately called for reservations at the coliseum. Since the Walk on Water concert would begin at seven in the evening and finish around ten, they decided to get a room and stay overnight and drive back in the morning. That night they were lucky enough to get the last room at the motel just across the road and between two restaurants. Willie wanted to go to the one that had breakfast all day and Rose wanted to go to the one with good service, serves good food, and have someone wait on her.

A young blond- haired policeman sat at the table next to Willie and Rose. He told them to be careful, very careful. Charlotte was a town of robbers and killers, thieves and con artists. He told them so much that he scared the Devil out of them. He pointed out, "Trust nobody, stay out of alleys, find a way to hide your money. Don't be alone, stay around people."

As seven o'clock approached, Willie and Rose got in the long line and were ushered to wonderful seats. The program started with a very funny comedian, followed by nine Johnson girls. The Walk on Waters were the greatest gospel singers in the world. The people that never had seen them should be forced to listen to them. There would be peace in the entire world. Willie could not count all the people who saw the Walk On Waters. He figured about three hundred, maybe a few more. Over 12 thousand, after the tickets were counted.

Several police officers were assigned duty to control the traffic and make sure the people who came from all over the state and South Carolina would be safe. Willie and Rose hurried to beat the traffic of people. As they neared the motel, Willie pulled at Rose's arm. He wanted to take one of his shortcuts he was famous for.

"Willie, we can't go behind the motel. That young Policeman told us about robbers and killers here in Charlotte. Let's walk in front where all the lights are."

Willie shook his head, "It is the side door not the rear door. You think I'm stupid or something."

Maybe she did not think him stupid, or just a little stupid. The two men that grabbed him knew he was stupid. They just beat the tar out of him, pulled him up with his legs and emptied his pockets. They turned to Willie and scooped up three-dollars and twenty-seven cents. They found another two dollars in his side pocket.

"That is all we wanted. You put up too much of a struggle for just five dollars." The tall one of the two turned to Rose.

"You mean that was all you wanted, just five dollars?"

"Yes, ma'am." The short one smug robber spoke up.

"Well, I wished I had knowed that was all you wanted. He thought you wanted them two-one hundred dollar bills he had in his shoes."

One Saturday morning after all the wise men met with Coca Colas, those little square nabs, and a fresh topic to spend the day at Deaton's Hardware and Feed Supply, Willie came in nearly out of breath.

"Come in and join the gang," Ross Jackson said.

Willie shook his head and said, "I gotta have a yard stick and quick."

Richard Deaton, owner and manager of the hardware store, ran over and helped Willie go through all the yardsticks.

"Is that the longest yardstick you have? I need a much longer yardstick. " Willie turned and headed for the door.

"I am sorry that I don't have any longer yardsticks."

It was Tuesday before Richard Deaton realized what happened. He finally got mad.

W illie and Walter were dragging an eight-point buck out of the woods when they ran across a couple of fellow hunters.

"Nice deer. Which of you got him?"

"Neither one. Leonard Harris shot him from his tree stand."

"Where's Leonard?" one of the two asked.

"He fell out of his tree stand. I think he broke his left leg. Took a bad fall too, he's trying to crawl out right now," Wille said as he continued to drag the deer out.

"You left Leonard with a broken leg and you are carrying the deer out. Why?"

"Well, we got to studying about it and we figured nobody would steal Leonard."

Uncle Willie stepped inside the post office to drop a couple of letters off. Both of his ears were wrapped in white bandages.

"My goodness, Willie, that looks like it hurts," The postmaster said.

"They really hurt. Take a while to get better."

"What in the world happened?"

"Rose was doing the ironing on the front porch Saturday night. She had the telephone on the end of the ironing board. The phone rang and I picked up the iron by mistake and pressed it against my right ear."

"What happened to your left ear?"

"The darned fool called back."

When the new fish camp opened on Little River, Willie and Rose decided they would stop by and see if it was a good place to eat. The whole town was bragging about the new eating place and had Rose excited. Friday night came and Willie was dressed and ready. Twenty minutes later Willie was pulling into the parking lot.

The hostess led them to a little alcove in the corner. It was almost romantic, appetites come first. Their waitress was a young lady from Troy. The food was ordered and within 15 minutes the seafood platters were set before Willie and Rose. Rose started eating. Willie sat back and smiled. The waitress came over and asked if everything was okay. Willie said it was. A few minutes later one of the other waitresses asked if there was something she could do for them. Again, Willie said that he was just fine and he was very happy.

Twice more the waitresses came over to Willie and smiled and asked what else they could get them. Again, no. Finally, the new manager came to Willie. "What is the problem, sir?"

"No, everything is very good."

"Why aren't you eating?"

"Rose has got the teeth now. I'll wait for my turn."

Willie and Rose were walking toward Morgan's Shoe Store and Used Furniture Store, when they saw Floyd Green coming and stopped to greet him. Floyd started to step aside, realized who they were, and quickly held his hand out to shake with Willie. "I was about to not recognize you two. I see that both of you are still healthy."

"Well, I see you haven't aged." Willie smiled and shook hands with Floyd.

"Oh, I wish I could look the same. I have really started to forget things."

"Goes with the aging. I guess we all are not as sharp as we used to be," Willie comforted Floyd.

"Oh no, this is a little scary. I would like to fill in the gaps."

"I went to the doctor and he gave me some pills. They worked miracles."

"That sounds great, Willie. What is the name of those pills?"

"I think I can help you out with that, Floyd. What is that flower that women like to grow? Most women have pretty gardens. Most of the time they are red."

"Do you mean a rose?" Floyd said.

"Yes, Rose. Rose, what was the name of those pills, what is the name the doctor gave me? It fixed me right up. Lloyd, I promise you will get your memories back."

W illie was sitting on the front porch where Rose was shelling beans. A car rolled up and a man stuck his head out the window.

"Can I take this road to Asheboro?" the man said.

"I don't care," Willie returned.

W illie and Vernon Haywood decided to go bear hunting. They packed their guns and ammo and a few things they were going to need and started out for Asheville. Willie told Rose he figured they would be back in four days. Vernon forgot to stop by his house and tell his wife good-bye.

Highway 40 was just a twinkle in the eye of a man somewhere up North. The trip was very long.

They stopped by the Pure Station and asked for a map of North Carolina. They were off. By the time they made it to Asheville it was nearly dark. The main roads through Asheville were easy to drive on and there were big signs every mile or so. Suddenly, Vernon struck his steering wheel with his fist.

"What is the matter?" Willie looked to Vernon.

"We might as well turn around and go home Willie."

"What happened?" Willie said.

"Take a look at that road sign."

There it was. Lit up bright and in large print. "Bear left."

"No use in staying. The bears left." Willie shook his head in disappointment.

It was a long drive home. Most service stations were closing and their banana sandwiches were getting soft.

F riday morning was busy at the bank with all the checks at the local mills paying off and the stores making sure there was enough change to cash checks and make change. The rush was over and there were just a couple in line. Leon Timken opened the door with a smile and let Willie in. As the two men entered and started toward the teller window, the front door shattered as if it was hit by a car. A man with wild eyes and a hungry look on his face came roaring in with a double-barreled shotgun.

"Everybody get on the floor and don't look at me. I want all the money from the bank and from all the money in people's pockets. I am not playing, I mean business."

Willie started wiggling around and trying to slide over towards Leon. Leon slid back towards the counter and tried to move away from Willie. Willie repeated his trying to get to Leon. Leon whispered and shook his head at Willie.

Willie was trying to hand something to Leon. He tried again. Finally, he was within less than an arms-length from Leon. Willie kept moving toward Leon. The bank robber had not noticed the actions of Willie. Leon had not missed the clinched right hand of Willie. With a loud whisper Leon asked Willie what was going on.

"Take this." Willie forced a piece of paper into Leon's left hand.

"What is it?" Leon whispered.

"It's the twenty dollars I borrowed from you last Friday."

D oc Craven opened the barber shop a little early. It was Saturday morning and the seats were already full and a line began to grow along the plastered wall. Usually, Doc would point to the silly large sign on the door. It said One Chair no waiting. For some reason it was going to be a busy day. Doc was an expert when it came to cutting hair. Zip, zip, and finished. Finished meant sweeping hair off with a whish broom, flipping his chair, and a palm of lavender water, and calling, "Next!"

By the time Willie made it to the chairs, there was a joke. It began with a giggle and as the men spoke up it was a buzzword. After a haircut, Doc offered a palm of his prized lavender water. The man getting out of the barber's chair repeated, when Doc said "You want me to slosh some of this lavender water on for you?"

"No, Doc, my wife would think that I had been in a house of ill repute."

No one could recall who said it first, but it drew laughs. Finally, Willie got his haircut and was rubbing his head to make sure he had any hair left.

"You want some of my lavender water?" Doc asked Willie.

"Yes sir, pour it on. My wife has never been in a house of ill repute. She would not know what they smell like."

I t was a beautiful day. There was not a cloud in the sky. Jesse Cole rolled his window down and laid his left arm on the door. Jesse was crossing the Pee Dee River bridge and headed towards Carthage. There was just a small curve and then the high hill on Highway 27. When he turned that little bit of a curve, he was shocked to see a very long line of cars. He figured it was a wreck, but then all the cars were in the right lane. The cars coming toward the Pee Dee bridge were passing as if nothing was happening up the road. He sat for a long time. Behind him a line of cars was getting longer and longer. He could stick his head out the window and every once in a while he could see a car dodge around something. Jesse changed his thinking from wreck to someone broke down.

He could see what the problem was. It was an older truck with silver toned sides and a door on the drivers' side that opened quickly and slammed again. It was his turn to be the car behind the old truck. The door opened again and to his surprise, out jumped Uncle Willie. He recognized Jesse, but stayed doing what he was doing. Aunt Rose jumped out with a broom in her hand.

"What in the world are you doing?" Jesse gasped.

"Ah, I got this truck full of chickens. I mean really full of chickens. This truck just does not have power enough engine to pull up this hill. I have to keep them flying so they weigh less. When I get to the station about two miles up the road, I'll stop and put a couple quarts of compression in. That should get us to Candor," Willie said.

"Get a broom and beat the sides of the truck to keep them chickens flying," Aunt Rose handed Jesse a worn out broom.

"I think you are going to put in more than two quarts of compression," Jesse said.

Uncle Willie was so bald-headed that he had to draw a line across his forehead to know when he needed to stop washing his face.

Willie and Rose stayed a little after the preacher had said amen for the last time. They had promised to take Flower Bell Hurley home. When he stomped on his starter, the only thing that happened was Flower Hurley jumped when she was startled. The preacher came running.

"What is the problem?" The preacher smiled as he approached Willie's car.

"I stepped on the starter and it just did not crank."

"Let me have a look at that motor. Raise the hood. I used to work at a garage when I was in high school." The preacher was as giddy as a 16- year -old with his first car.

Willie raised the hood, stepped back out of the preacher's way. The preacher smiled and leaned over with his arms at his belt line. His smile turned into a grin. The preacher changed sides to give himself a better look at the motor. Suddenly, the hood dropped right on top of the preacher's head. His chin hit his chest and he stumbled backwards.

The term widow's peak changed meaning. His right hand had to be pulled out by Willie. There was no damage to the hand, but it was skinned on the back of the knuckles. The preacher blew on the hand to cool it down. He turned in anger and seemed to be trying to curse. Willie, Rose, and Flower Bell saw the preacher's mouth get wider.

"You are not going to say bad words are you?" Willie said with a shaky voice.

"No, but if you write some bad words on a piece of paper, I will sign it."

W illie Jr. and a couple of his friends had played out that summer's evening. It was near sunset and the dust from the dirt road was lingering in the air. The lack of rain had the white dust seem like flour on the floor.

"Let's play snake." Willie Jr. said.

It was simple. The setting sun and the road was all they needed. A dark piece of rope, or a fan belt, or anything that could be pulled along and twist like something alive. This time a fan belt from an old car was perfect.

Sewing thread tied around the fan belt could not be seen by someone driving by. The white dust would hide markings on a snake. One boy would drag the make-believe snake across the road. It took two boys to gently make the snake come alive and crawl on the road. It was not a long wait. In less than ten minutes, the sound of a car could be heard. The snake was dropped and they eased the snake across the road.

It was the preacher. He had his headlights on and did not care if the dust swirled behind him.

He slid sideways and opened the car door. He ran towards Willie's house.

"Willie, get to the door and bring a shotgun with you. I just saw a 10 foot rattlesnake. I never seen such a big snake. Hurry."

In an old building somewhere near Candor, a limp little bit of fan belt lies. In the echoes of snake tales still heard in the laughter of old men who still remember the preacher's giant rattlesnake. From the piece of fan belt which still lies, to the preacher that still lies.

Willie's doctor told him to exercise and change his diet to wholesome food. "Do that or there would be a slow walking and a sad singing in the county."

Willie thought to himself, Fishing is exercise, deer hunting, rabbit hunting were exercise. But, so was walking, paddling his old boat was exercise. A bicycle was darn good exercise although he had not ridden a bike since he was a teenager. If he needed to eat wholesome food and work out with daily exercise, then Rose needed to join him. She cooked the food and sewed dresses, neither of those activities were real exercise. Rose had gained a whole bunch of weight in the last couple few years. He thought he would stop by Morgan's shoe store and used furniture. He found a bicycle built for two, nearly brand new. He tossed it in the back of his truck and headed home.

He managed to get out of the house without being seriously hurt. Rose stopped at the front door and threw a fire poker straighter than Jim Bowie could throw his knife. She would not ride a bicycle due to the fact she only wore frocks, she would not wear peddle- pushers. If Willie said one more word about her riding a bicycle, she would aim that fire poker dead center and he would never sit in a chair again. His old buddy, Roy Harris, would be interested in riding anything.

Willie and Roy became addicted to a morning ride around Candor and they even made a few trips to Norman. All those destinations were on level ground, they wanted adventure, excitement, to have people brag about them. They were after thrills.

About three miles out of Candor was Loving Hill. It lived up to its name. The history went back to the American War for Independence. There were rattlesnakes and copperheads all over the top of the hill. There was even a family that made the best white liquor. Down another road was a church and a set of high hills. But, the biggest hill was at the New Hospital at Troy. After they rode that far and then rode a bicycle to the top of the Hospital, that would make them heroes.

Of course they picked a hot day in July. Even the black gnats had to walk; it was too hot to fly. They were already soaking wet from sweat and tired from pumping up tires and oiling the brakes. They rode in the middle of the road in Troy. They wanted to make everyone aware of what was going to happen.

Willie was the brains of this stunt. That was scary onto itself, but Roy Harris considered himself the master in bikes and pedals and handlebars, brakes and brutal bars. He was about five foot six and built like a tank. He misunderstood nearly everything that was said to him.

The two men began riding the bicycle built for two almost exactly one P.M.

"Keep going no matter how slow and don't let it roll backwards." That was Willie's words of wisdom to Ray.

Slowly the two men made their way up the high hill. Willie seemed the most tired of the two men. There were several times that the bike stood still until Willie regained his breath. Finally, they made it to the top.

"I thought we would never make it to the top. I was afraid the bike would roll back. We could have been hurt," Willie said between gasps of breath.

"I knew that would not happen. I kept the brakes on all the way to the top," Roy said with pride and a smile.

The preacher's wife called him to the telephone. He asked her who was calling. She said it was the IRS. He lost most of his breath and his legs began to tremble. He mumbled something that sounded like he dreaded this day. His voice got sweet, and he was smiling when the voice on the phone wanted to check on one of his members. Willie and Rose said that they had tithed 500 dollars for the year. The preacher told the tax collector that he was not sure if Willie had given that amount of tithing, but he promised that Wille would.

B utch Hall was not a good neighbor, man, husband, or anything else a man needed to be. He did go to church Sunday, but he snorted, made scary faces to the children, and sang so out of tune the choir were talking of tar and feathers. There was a story about his wife having to hold a pistol on Butch so he could shave without cutting his own throat. The more people got to know him, the more they believed that little story.

Butch bragged about his dog, Devil. Devil was a Doberman pinscher with a serious attitude. Butch fed Devil twice a day. With store bought food with tabasco added. And in the evening, gunpowder was mixed with what was left in the morning. The dog was very mean, and the hot pepper and gunpowder made him meaner with ulcers. Butch would enter the dog fight down Capelise way. Every Saturday evening, men paid good money to watch a dog die. Devil was an attraction as he tore the throat of a family pet.

Catfish McIntyre made a white liquor run to lower Georgia. He brought back what he said was the end of Devil. It was a secret and the dog was hidden away. Willie had heard Devil would be a memory after Saturday night. There was a lot of money passed and all the law enforcement in three counties drove in just to see the fight.

When the men turned into the road where the dog fight would be held, the usual twenty-five watt light bulb was not on. Getting out of the car was difficult. A storm had knocked off power in the surrounding neighborhood. And the heavy rains had made the driveway almost impossible. There were Coleman lanterns and cattails soaked in kerosene for lights. The night sky still threatened more storms.

Devil, the fiercest dog of the night, was at his best. He jumped the short wall to get to the other dog. Flashlights, candles, and car lights pointed at it. Devil growled and attacked whatever there was to fight. Suddenly all noise stopped from the dog pit. There was one loud scream and again more silence. Butch grabbed someone's flashlight and with a stout walking stick he jumped into the fight. He screamed and ran away. People were confused and frightened. Cars spun in the mud. Some of the men thought that the police were arresting men that showed up at the dog fight. Catfish McIntyre stood tall and unafraid. He even sneered at Butch as Butch found the highway, found the middle of it and took off running.

Willie walked over to Catfish and both stared into the dog pit. There was something moving around, it was not Devil. Devil had pointed ears, slanted eyes, and teeth like a chainsaw. Devil did not jump out of the dog pit. There was nothing left of him. Catfish leaned over the dog pit and shook his head.

"What was that? What happened?" Willie could not grasp what Catfish McIntyre did.

"Well, the neighborhood bully is no more. Butch has had enough. When I got back from Georgia, I brought an alligator back with me. I painted it orange and cut its tail off. It was not a dog."

There was a special service Sunday. Even though it was not Easter, the church was full. The preacher won Preacher of the Year for the whole state. He had been named top Baptist. It would have been a slap in the face to the preacher, an insult to him and his entire family if the church was not packed. Willie and Rose had to go. There could be no alibis, no sore throats, colds, or hangovers.

Willie and Rose talked about what time they should walk through the doors of the church. Get there late and sit on the back row and then get up and out after the preacher prayed the last prayer. Get there early and everyone would see the lumps on his head and the dark areas around his eyes and forehead. Willie looked like he challenged Rocky Marciano to a fist fight.

Everyone, even the small children and very old women, could not take their eyes off of him. Even the preacher had that,

what-in-the-hell-grabbed-a-hold-of-you, look on
his face. Willie seemed to draw more of an audi-
ence than the preacher with his little 4 inch by 6
inch, wrapped in paper, state made picture to sit on
desk. Willie had had practiced most of the night. He
had made hand motions to make it more dramatic.

"It looked like any other Saturday. The lawn was
mowed and planted a few roses. About one o'clock
Rose wanted to ride up to Asheboro to do a little
shopping. Then there was a little mistake. Someone
crawled on a horse. It was an old man getting older
but he looked like he thought he could ride him. He
busted loose and tossed me sideways. He was fast
and nearly threw the rider off. The saddle slipped
on a stirrup and nearly slid off. The rider was really
taking a beating."

"Willie was lucky, he could have been the hurt
bad," Rose spoke up loudly.

"What stopped him from being hurt?" one of the
deacons turned to look at Rose.

"The manager of the Grant Store ran out and
unplugged the horse. The manager and me pulled
Willie off safely. He took a lot of bumps," Rose said.

"I would like to get my hands on the kid that put
that quarter into that machine," Willie moaned.

R ose was really happy. She wanted to ride up to Cherokee on the church bus. Ten of the older women in the church decided that they were going to leave Thursday morning, spend the night at the River Motel, stay all day Friday and climb back on the church bus early enough to make it back home around six o'clock Saturday evening. There was only one motel and nothing to see other than a river, and tourist souvenirs. Sometime on Friday afternoon, a Bible study will complete a young Indian woman's address to the women. Rose had never been that far from home or traveled that long in a bus. She really dreaded leaving Willie. Willie could get into trouble locked in a room full of preachers.

Around seven o'clock Rose called Willie to make sure that everything was okay. He answered the telephone and was glad to hear Rose's voice. After finding out that Willie was well, she asked about how her pet cat was.

"Your cat is dead," Willie loudly snapped out.

"Willie, that was terrible. You should have broke that bad news slowly."

"How should I have given the bad news to you.?"

"You should have told me the cat was on the roof. Then you could have called me and tell me the cat fell off the roof. Later you could have called me and said the cat was dead. You should have broke the bad news slowly. By the way, Willie how is mama?"

"She's on the roof."

B ack when Jinx Morgan was running a sawmill out on Whiskey Road, it seemed that Willie only worked four days a week. Jinx lived about a half a mile from the sawmill, and Willie and Rose lived just beyond him. There were five workers at the sawmill and one snaked the logs out of the forest. Monday was the day most likely for Willie to lay out. Jinx put up with Willie because he was a very good worker when he did go to work.

Monday morning found Willie knocking on Jinx's door. He was sick with a sore throat and both feet hurt. Willie told Jinx he would be at work Tuesday unless his feet hurt him. Willie started the fire for his wife to boil the water and do the wash. At about noon Rose told Willie she was out of bluing and soap for the wash. He might as well go pick those items up so he started out walking to town. He had to pass the sawmill where all the workers were eating lunch and he would put up for Jinx.

Willie was right, all the men hooted and hollered at him. Jinx stood up and yelled out for Willie to stop and tell him a lie. Willie kept running. Jinx called out for Willie for just one lie. Willie turned his head back and said he could not stop, Jinx's wife had been bitten by a big rattle snake and he was going to get the doctor. He kept running. Jinx ran up the road screaming.

Later that afternoon Willie walked back to his front yard. He handed Rose the washing soap. Jinx was there and he was just a little angry.

"Willie, you like to have give me a heart attack. I ran all the way home and my wife said she had not been bit by a snake. Did not even see one."

"Well, you told me to tell you a lie."

W illie and Leon were riding through Abner. Suddenly the front left tire popped and that side of the car started to rattle. Leon climbed out of the passage side and began rolling up his shirt sleeves. Willie began pulling some of the wildflowers and placing them at the front of the car and then did the same for the rear of the car.

"What are you doing, Willie? What are you doing?" Leon shook his head.

"I seen this on television. When you have a flat tire you have to have flowers at the front of the car and flowers at the rear of the car."

"I think they meant flares."

The preacher was in the spirit and was going overtime. Willie was nodding off and having a hard time staying awake. Finally, he dropped off to sleep. He was bad to snore and beginning to bother the people near him.

The preacher turned his head towards Willie and Rose. "Miss Rose, if you would, please wake Mr. Willie."

Rose folded her arms. "Why don't you wake him up, you put him to sleep?"

W illie listened for any sound that would tell him the Game Warden was in the woods. A snap from a dry limb or animal running away would give the Game Warden away. He had heard a heavy foot trying to sneak up to him. Willie was fishing without a license and had six of the biggest catfish he had ever caught. He was trying to ease the fish into the water, so the Game Warden would not give him a ticket. Suddenly, there was a cloud of dust and a mighty, "I got you!" coming from a large oak tree.

"I finally caught you, Willie. It has been a long time coming, but I got you red-handed."

"You still ain't got me. I ain't hunting and I ain't fishing."

"What do you call them in the bucket?" The officer in green said with a little too much pride.

"These? Oh, I guess they are like any catfish, but I went to Hoffman and got a dozen of these trained catfish. They are hand trained for a fish show in Florida." Willie smiled.

"I never heard of a fish show in Florida."

"Me and Rose drove down to Florida to sign some legal papers. We are putting up our life's savings into this venture."

"Boy, I never knew that. Can you train those cat-fish?"

"That is what I am doing here. I train six at the time, and I then tip the bucket over very easy-like. I let them exercise in the creek and then I pick them up and take them home," Willie said, trying to keep a straight face.

"And they know to come back here?"

"It will take about 20 minutes. Let's go sit on that tree stump."

Time passed. The Game Warden sat in awe about the trained fish. Suddenly Willie got up and re-trieved his bucket and said goodbye to his green dressed friend.

"Here now, if I didn't know you, I'd think you was just messing with me."

"Where is your evidence? You can't take me to jail with an empty bucket."

"You won't fool me again. I can promise that."

"There is a deer at the house that committed suicide, gotta skin her out before dark."

The regular preacher brought an honored guest to speak on the evils of alcohol. The guest himself spent twelve years as prisoner to wine, beer, rotgut white liquor and under arm deodorant if you used that brand. He wasn't a tall man, or fat man. He smiled with a smile from earlobe to earlobe. He held the Bible with a firm grip. The first thing he did was to reach under the pulpit and pull out a mason jar half filled with clear water, white liquor, and pink fishing worms. He set the jar down and started preaching.

About an hour later, the honored guest reached over and picked up the mason jar. He held it high. He shook it and held it hit again. There were ahs and awes throughout the church.

"Brothers and Sisters, I went up to a local liquor house and bought a jar of real alcohol. I put water and worms with evil whiskey and now look at them. The worms are dissolved into soup. Look at that jar and what it does. Tell me what you think."

Willie raised his hands. "Well, it proves to me that if you drink alcohol, you won't have worms."

It was a normal Saturday. Willie was stretched out on what was left of the sofa watching Killer Jenkins take on all the wrestling stars. Rose was taking the apple pie out of the oven and little Willie Junior was in the front yard playing Davy Crockett. He used a tobacco stick for his rifle. Tobacco sticks were full of splinters, so he was careful. There was a loud scream followed by a louder scream. Then Willie Junior stomped through the house and then screamed again.

Willie jumped off the sofa and ran straight into the door. Rose slammed the oven door. "What happened?" Willie shouted.

"I seen a bear. A big bear on the porch!" Willie Junior screamed again.

"Both of you get in the closet. I'll try to scare the bear off," Willie said as he loaded his shotgun. Willie was not out of the house in less than five minutes. "Boy that is not a bear. That is a big dog."

Willie Junior looked around. "I thought it was a bear."

"Boy, you get in your bedroom and pray to Jesus and ask for forgiveness for telling a lie."

Willie shook his head and turned up the Killer Jenkins on television. In less than five minutes, Willie Junior came out of his bedroom and started outside.

"I thought I told you go into your room and ask Jesus for forgiveness."

"I already got that from Jesus. He said when he saw that dog, he thought it was a bear."

Willie, Rose, and Leon Timken drove up to Raleigh to tour the State Fair. Rose loved to ride the rides. Her favorite was the Wild Mouse. Leon enjoyed walking around and seeing the animals and the new farm equipment. Willie was a sucker for the spiels by the men dressed in brown suits and black shoes. One man had a large cage with five parrots that seemed to be identical. They jumped from one birch to another, then jumped back again. Their rasping almost growling changed from a crow to a buzzard.

The spiel man at that booth nodded for Willie to step over and get a good look at the parrots. Willie jumped at that opportunity with glee. He always wanted a parrot. He smiled. The spiel man reached in and brought one of the parrots out. He set the parrot on a long piece of wood shaved like a broom handle.

"What is your name?" The spiel man had a sucker and knew it.

"Willie is my name, but most folks call me Uncle Willie."

"Well, Uncle Willie, step up here and let me show you how easy it is to train one of these birds."

The man leaned over and with a gentle stroke from the top of the parrot's head to the middle of his back. "Say, Uncle Willie. Say Uncle Willie."

The parrot walked up the stick, bobbled his head a few times then spoke clearly. "Uncle Willie, Uncle Willie."

"Rose, I just had to buy that parrot. It was so easy to train. It did not take five minutes to have it talking. I want to teach it a lot."

"Willie, you know, and I know that man as good as stole that money from you. It is a trick. He could throw his voice, or had something electric to fool you with."

"I think he really taught that parrot to talk. He has been doing this for years. Me and Willie trained Blue Tick Hounds and I think—" Leon said and was cut off by Rose.

"Leon, if you had one intelligent thought, it would go to your head and die of loneliness. I still say that the parrot was some kind of a trick. But, I'll let Willie have it and try to get it to talk. It is a cute parrot and we will call it Polly, just like the one on the Jack Benny show."

Willie had bought a parrot cage, four bags of parrot food, a little mirror to hang in the cage, and a small booklet on how to train birds. He was like a kid putting the parrot in the cage and started trying to teach it to say Uncle Willie. He said, "Say Uncle Willie," about a thousand times and the parrot never opened his mouth. Over and over the same thing was repeated. Over and over again the parrot just stood there and once in a while it would turn its head sideways. Willie covered the cage with a dish towel and turned out the kitchen lights.

Saturday morning came and nothing from Polly. The day got old and the parrot had to listen to Uncle Willie nearly all day. Nothing but the silence from the parrot in the kitchen. Willie left the towel off and the kitchen lights off. When Rose woke up and went into the kitchen, she called Willie to hurry to the kitchen. The door to the cage was open and the cage was empty. The window over the sink had been left half open and a few feathers were still on the open window.

Willie dressed and ran outside. He heard panic from all the chickens. Some ran around, some found a hiding place. He ran inside the barn and to the call of a rooster or the parrot. When he got to the rear door, he saw the parrot holding on to the rooster. With his left wing the parrot held the rooster against the door and the right wing held the rooster. Willie heard the sound and quickly understood it.

The parrot would punch the rooster and say "Uncle Willie. Say Uncle Willie." And he kept saying it. Willie decided to keep the parrot.

There was a sign about four feet by four feet and painted by hand hanging from a tree limb. It said, *Watch your melons and count your lopes*.

Willie always had a big field for watermelons and cantaloupe and knew how to use them. He never sold a watermelon before the fourth of July to make sure they were ripe. Cantaloupe came in several different sizes. He had a major problem with local kids sneaking off with several watermelons. He had slept on his front porch to catch the melon thieves. They were smart and he could not catch them. He even fired his double-barreled shotgun into the air just to scare them.

Willie was getting angry and really wanted the thieves to stop. He had a brainstorm. He waited until it was dark and he put another sign up. He was aided by being Saturday night. Sunday morning came and he slipped his shoes on and went outside. There it hung and it was very good. He had Herman Smith to paint the sign. It said, *There is one poison melon and I am the only one who knows where it is.* His smiling ended, his mouth dropped over and his eyes had to read the sign. There was another sign. It was simple, but effective. *Uncle Willie, be careful eating your melons. You know where a poisoned melon is and we know where the other one is.*

W illie answered his front door and there stood Bob Brown. Bob was the type of man that went to work, came home, went to church, and came home. It was not that he was so religious, it was the fact that he married the meanest woman in the county. Well, a couple of the counties. She looked like Popeye the Sailor, complete with the little pipe Popeye always carried. Her name was Vitalee. Vitalee came from Robinson County and somehow she managed to get Poor Little Bob across the state line and married him one rainy day in Chester, South Carolina. That was about all that ever happened in their rather dull life.

Bob Brown and Willie sat down and talked about Bob's problem. Just one problem. Vitalee was jealous. She was always afraid she was going to lose her man. Bob had given up on a good wife and surrendered to Vitalee. Recently, she began to really put the pressure on him, thinking that he was seeing other women. She made Poor Little Bob stop at the front door and she would inspect him, even taking his coat off and she checked him for lipstick or the aroma of some thought up perfume.

Willie had the answer to Poor Little Bob's problem. So simple and yet so perfect. Willie told Poor Little Bob to brush off his trousers, clean his shoes off, and take his coat off and shake it off dust, lint, and more importantly hair. It was genius and both men agreed it would work. About a week later Willie heard what could be called shy rap on the front door. Outside waiting for him stood Poor Little Bob. Bob had a large bandage covering his nose. Another bandage was carefully placed on his left eye.

"What happened to you?" Willie said with a startled expression on his face.

"You done me wrong, Willie. You give me the wrong advice."

"How? I thought it was good."

"Well, I followed your directions exactly. I even took the coat off and shook it hard. When I went into the house my wife circled me for ten minutes. She punched me in the nose and said that I had stooped to running with bald headed women."

Willie met John Young, alias John Yammanitz, alias Charlie Rossie, at the drug store in Candor over a hot cup of coffee. John Young, at the time, was taking a day to sell Bibles. If he did not make his quota, he was going to spend the night at the motel. He was tall, well built, handsome, and gifted with a talent that could sell ice to an Eskimoux. His voice was as smooth as good white liquor and his heart was as black as midnight in a cave. In thirty-minutes, he had Willie hired to drive him around town. Willie knew everyone and knew where they lived and what church they attended. John put three large boxes in the back seat and the trunk of his car. Off the merry twosome went.

John Young was at his best and usually sold two Bibles to one family. Willie made suggestions on who to sell to and who to speed away as quick as they could. John wore a good suit, he dressed to impress, and with that Northern accent he was doing well. His accent sometimes made people mad.

Then it was time to drive off. John also smoked fancy cigars that gave him a sophisticated look. The day was going perfect and there was a lot of sunlight left. John had a little speech he used to clinch a sale. "If a man comes in your house to steal your money, hide your money in the Bible. A thief will not look through your Bible. If someone opens your Bible to read it and finds the money you put there, they will not steal your money. It is the safest safe in the world."

At one house, John could see the lady living there as they turned into the driveway. She had long blonde hair. She smiled. She invited Willie and John to enter the house. She had a knack at decoration and her house was the cleanest and best kept he had seen. That did not say that the others were not as clean or anything, it was that the young bride was the prettiest girl John had ever seen. Ten minutes into his spiel, the young lady ordered three of the Bibles. She wanted one for herself and one for her mother and one for her mother-in-law. It was at that time that a man stepped in. He was tall, with both arms looking like an ox. It happened so quick that John did not know he had lost the sale. Somewhere between hello and goodbye, John found himself walking down the steps of the porch with Willie. The man was the husband of the blonde. Her husband did not want the Bibles. That was the end of it.

The rest of the sales day was very good. John Young and Willie sat at the best table of the Court Hotel and counted the Bibles that were sold. It was not even five-o'clock. The steaks were good and all that was missing was a good wine. There was no legal purchase to be bought in the county.

John stopped and asked Willie to take him back to where the beautiful blonde lived. If her husband was not at home, John knew the blonde would buy at least three Bibles and maybe a few more.

"I had rather not to go back there. Skin Brown is a very dangerous man," Willie explained.

"We will get in and out so quick, she won't know what hit her."

"I am afraid you won't know what hit you. I will stay in the car."

"That's even better. These little Southern gals may be pretty, but they are dumber than a nanny goat. Just stay in the car and honk the horn if you see her husband coming and if you don't see him coming, don't come in the house," John said with the old yankee wink of his eye.

***

"Are you okay?" Willie shook John and he heard a rattle.

"I won't be ok again in my life," John said as he attempted to brush the dust off.

"I heard about Skin but until this very moment I had never seen him get mad," Willie puffed between breaths.

"Is he gone?"

"I did not see him come up. I heard you squeal like a woman and I saw you flying over the front porch."

John tried to stand, but he was still wobbly. "Give me a minute to shake off this dizzy head and I will go back in the house and show Skin a couple of things."

"All that happened an hour ago. Skin and his Darling left to eat at the Court. I am glad you won't fight him. Besides, he has a very bad dog he keeps under the front porch. That dog is a mean dog. We can leave now."

John finally stood and he turned to the passenger door. He bit down on his cigar and took a draw hoping to wake him up. "Mean dog?"

"Yeah, a mean dog. One of them with a long nose and pointed ears. John, that ain't a cigar you got in your mouth."

***

"What did he do?" Leon asked.

"Oh, he tried to spit it out. I bet he is still gagging and spitting." Willie said with an ear to ear smile .

"Was you hurt? I heard you were driving the car."

"I was not hurt. I still have nightmares that keep me awake. Doc Simmons said he would recommend that I see one of those head doctors. They got some good ones at Raleigh. I don't think I need therapy, it will take some time, but I will get over it. John might not get over it. Last week the preacher talked about a savage hell that John endured.

The Preacher was having a good service. Everything was going fine, but when he looked over to his right, he realized that Willie and Rose were not in their normal pew. That was the third straight week they missed church. It bothered him that two of his lambs might need help. He made a note to himself to visit Willie and Rose. Monday afternoon, the preacher got out of his love offering new car. He tapped on the front door and was given a warm welcome. After a cup of coffee and home-made cake, the preacher got down to business.

"I hope you two are doing well. I am worried about your health, in these times you never know when you pick up a virus or even a sprain or break a leg," the preacher said, leaning forward and smiling.

"Me and Rose are doing well. There have been a few lazy days, but we will get going."

"Bless your hearts, the both of you. I have not seen you and your lady for a few weeks. Is there something I can do to help you?'"

"Well, preacher, I am ashamed to say it, but Willie and me don't have good clothes. I had rather stay home than embarrass ourselves by holes in sweaters or shoes all raggedy and Willie does not have a decent white shirt for Sunday."

"Bless your hearts. Neither of you should be embarrassed when I am around. I growed up as poor as a church mouse, but I followed that mouse to college and from college to study how to teach the Lord's word. I am going to preach Wednesday at prayer meeting about love and love offerings. Your names will not be brought up."

"We would be real happy if you did that." Rose smiled a joyous smile of acceptance.

Thursday morning came around and two of the nicest deacons pulled up in Willies' driveway. Coffee was served and the love offering was counted out and a ride to Troy was offered to Willie and Rose.

About three weeks later the preacher knocked on Willies' door. The preacher shook hands and sat down at the kitchen table. "Well, did you get the love offerings?"

"Oh yes," Rose and Willie spoke up at the same time.

"Well, did you buy the clothes?"

"Yes, they are beautiful. We are so proud of them," Willie said.

"Well, I haven't seen you at church lately."

"Preacher, to tell the truth, we put them clothes on and we decided they made us look so good, we started going to the Presbyterian church," Willie confessed.

Leon Timken staggered out of the barroom with Willie dragging behind him. The air was so fresh that both men stopped for a few minutes on the bench. Then they walked to where Leon's was parked under dim light. Leon opened the driver side and plopped down taking a deep breath. Willie followed and pulled him door tight.

"Go call the sheriff, Willie. Look, some bad boys have tore out the steering wheel and all the good stuff. "

"I'm a going, quick as I can."

When Willie closed the door behind him, he reached for the wall telephone. Leon was yelling for Willie to hang up the telephone.

"What's the matter? "

"Willie, we sat down in the back seat. Don't call the sheriff, he might think we have been drinking."

Willie and little Willie sat in the chairs that were placed there for tired shoppers. Rose had just begun to shop. Willie was tired and his feet hurt. Not only that, but Rose had the checkbook. Willie only shopped in that clothing store a few times. Things would change and that thrilled him. There was the x-ray machine that when stepped on showed the feet and gave the exact size for shoes. For some reason, the store stopped using that machine. Now they had another machine that Willie just could not figure out. There was a half telephone booth, a person could go inside and after a few minutes they would come out different.

Willie was taking a break for shopping so he could watch the new machine. First there was an older lady who just walked right up, pushed a little black button. A few minutes later the door opened and a gorgeous blonde stepped out. Again and again Willie watched one person turn into another person. He asked a woman passing by what that was. She told him it was an elevator.

He told Willie Jr. to go find his mother. Willie said he wanted to run her through that door before they went home.

It was nearly dark when Willie heard the loud screams and cursing coming from Bill Yarburro's direction. At first, Willie thought Bill was calling in his cows and whatever needed to come in for the night. It was louder than that, so Willie got Rose to ride over to Bill and see what was going on. Bill was up in the hay loft and still screaming and making loud sounds. Bill was holding onto a length of hemp rope and standing close to the barn doors.

"What in the world are you up to?" Willie shouted out to Bill.

"I am a suiciding myself. You and Rose don't need to see this horrible thing I am doing!" Bill shouted down to Willie.

Bill was wrapping the hemp rope around his legs and chest. In an instant, Bill jumped and was dangling between the ground and the hay loft. Willie stepped out of his car and reached for Bill who was too high to bring down. Willie was getting angry at

Bill and found a long stick to push Bill back and forth.

"Bill, this is silly. You are swinging like a monkey. Why are you doing this?"

"Lucile said she was going to leave me. I ain't got no life now."

"Lucile left you twenty times this year. I don't think you need to drink as much as you do. In fact, I did not know you drank until you showed up at the church sober one time. You are all tied up in that rope. Why not wrap that rope around your neck and get this suicide over with."

"I already tried that, I could not breathe. I had to stop that."

L ittle Bet was the best mule in the county. Willie was so proud of her that he bragged to all the hunters who came over to see the miracle of a mule. Little Bet was always ready to go on a hunt. No matter what she was after, Little Bet stayed on the hunt. She took the hunters straight up to the rabbit, squirrel, deer, it did not matter. Willie said when they were hunting raccoons or possums Little Bet would tree them just like a Blue Tick Hound. He said he had seen her turn around and mule kick the tree until the raccoon or possum fell out.

Grady Baxter and Albert Britt had heard all the wild tales Willie was smiling and spreading around. They drove all the way from Norman to see for themselves how good a mule would chase rabbits. They pulled into Willie's driveway at 8·45 A.M. and started unloading their shotguns and hunting boots. Grady did all the talking. Willie was not expecting the duo, but met them with a smile.

"Boys, I have to do some things this morning and one of them is to take my wife to the food store. I will be back around one. So if you want to come back, I will be glad to take you down and show you the only hunting mule in the state."

"I wish we could come back today, but we are having a big outdoor cookout at the church. We have to be back around five. We are all filled up at the furniture store for the rest of the month. We would really like to see your mule hunt."

"I believe I can trust both of you men, I am going to let you go down and hunt with Little Bet and bring her back and put her up. She has never met a stranger and she listens real good. Take her on down. I hope I get back soon enough to see what you kill."

"Thank you, Mr. Willie and I can promise you we will take good care of her."

"I hate to leave you, but like I said I got to get to town. If you want to, I'll open the gate for Little Bet and you and your buddy can follow her down to the creek. Down west of the creek there will be a bright blue rag up on the barbed wire fence. Turn and go down stream until you find a hill, turn right there and follow it back to the gate and lock Little Bet in and double the gate."

"Is that far to walk? Will the mule run on us?"

"Not Little Bet, she won't run. Just follow her and you will get all the rabbits you want."

"Really? This I have to see." Grady turned and watched Little Bet as she just stood there.

***

When Willie and Rose returned from their shopping, he noticed the car that the two men drove up from Norman in. He turned his head towards the mule's gate. Then he saw both men sitting in the wooden lawn chairs.

"You fellows been sitting there long?" Willie asked.

"We took Little Bet straight down there. You might have been five minutes up the road. We found that blue rag and made a turn up stream. She is just down there. We could not get her in her fence. We did not want to leave her out. We were afraid she would wander off."

"When you made that turn up stream was a mistake. I really appreciate you waiting for me to get back. You could have left her out, she would come home. But, when you went down by the creek she just stopped. She loves to fish a lot more than she likes to hunt. She will be back with a string of fish."

Willie heard some kind of noise. He jumped up out of bed and grabbed his trusty shotgun and eased his way down the hall. At the end of the hall, where Rose had a mirror and a flower vase, there was movement, then a shadowy evil face. There he saw a strange man looking at him. He ran towards the strange man trying to pin him against the wall. Willie realized he was out of breath, he was overweight, with limp almost soggy arms. He slipped and landed on his back, the horrible sound from crashing on the floor and into the mirror, scattered all the flowers and splashed water all over him.

Little Willie Jr. jumped out of bed to join the fight. He crashed his baseball bat into the man on the floor. Rose saw the man on the floor and she grabbed her Bible with both hands and struck the intruder five times with a ten pound Bible.

After, Willie put his bathrobe on and had six cups of the strongest coffee in the county, he began to unravel the goings on at the family home. He had seen his own reflection in the mirror, but he had not recognized himself. Willie Jr. said he had not recognized his own father. Rose said she was too frightened to see who it was breaking mirrors and spilling flowers and water. That night he would take a vow to slim down and he was starting right then.

For breakfast, instead of four eggs, a large plate of sausage, four biscuits and white gravy, Willie ate one egg and grits. Times had changed in the family kitchen. Rose was amazed when Willie set out on a walk around the backyard. He drove up to main street and went inside the drug store. He bought all the women's magazines because they carried articles on how to lose weight and what to eat and what not to eat. The Almanacs all had ads for what one needed to work-out and take the weight off. Six weeks later, Willie received the last of his mail orders. He had already lost two pounds on his own, now with all these professional machines and working out equipment, he was ready to be called "Slim" again.

Rose was just a little angry that Willie had bought over four hundred dollars' worth of health food and enough scrap iron to build an airplane. Some of the cheaper purchases had all been returned to the companies or too torn up to use. The chin bar that went on the hall door was as dangerous as an angry rattlesnake. When he screwed the chin bar in and he pulled himself up by his hands, with the palms of his hands pointing towards his face, he tried to pull himself twice. When he put his weight behind it there was an evil snap in the bar. Willie hit the floor and the bar looked like a V.

Never throw something when mad. Willie learned that right then. He was standing at the front door, he threw the screen door wide open and he grabbed the V and tossed it as far as he could. As far as he could throw it was nearly half- way in the front yard. Joe Dog was coming in after a night of lewd and wild howling. He was not in the mood for V shaped cheap aluminum boomerangs. Willie was lucky to get the door shut before Joe Dog came through it looking for blood or brains. The V shaped rod hit the front door breaking three windows.

One of Willie's set- backs was the miracles of the diet pills. For five dollars, he could buy twenty-four pills that taken one a day would guarantee weight loss. He walked right into that one. After six days, he opened the lid to take his morning pill. The whole bottle was crawling with worms, thin, black worms. He lost weight for two days. Worse, Willie Jr. took the worms down to the creek and caught three fish. Willie Senior had to eat a spoonful of sugar and one drop of turpentine every day for a week. No one could strike a match around him.

Willie Senior, strung the spare room with rubber innertube and a lot of the red rubber. He wove them and worked out every day. It was a great room, but he seemed to not be losing the weight he needed. He found one work out book that impressed him. That book would be the one he needed. He liked the way the rubber stretched and he used the big round balls. He started with a ball about the size of a soft ball. Then each week he used a little larger and heavier. He was sitting across the room and had the ball in one rubber band that he connected to the door. He rigged it up so the doorknob would be held until he turned it loose. He could turn it loose. Him, not any another person.

Rose forgot. On her way to yell, "Soup's on", Rose forgot again and opened the precious door with the hard rubber ball twelve feet away from Willie. There was no alarm given, none of that "heads up" or anything. Willie Junior figured the speed from the door to Willie's forehead to be fifty-eight miles an hour, give or take a couple of miles.

The hard rubber ball ricocheted off of Willie's forehead, hit the ceiling, bounced to the floor, and back into Willie's forehead. That was a storm he managed to weather. He almost forgave Rose for the two knots on his forehead. He had rathered Willie Jr. opened the door. That way he could blame a mere child and he did not want to blame his wife.

One of the early arrivals of the weight loss program was all about balls. There was a medicine ball and something that looked like a bowling ball. He was to toss them around on a sheet of red rubber until he built up muscles in his arms. He got the knack of tossing the balls and catching them. He used his head on mounting the balls. He had learned his lesson about red rubber and small hard rubber tied around one of those glass doorknobs. For this ingenious idea, Willie ran an old well water pulley through a series of rubber bands. If the door were opened the medicine ball would instantly shoot up towards the ceiling and then slowly drop to the floor.

When the automobile was being invented, there were a lot of things to correct. Same thing with the first airplanes. Willie's floor to the ceiling medicine ball needed at least two more days before perfection. When Rose howled, "Soup's on" and the door opened, the medicine ball hit the ceiling (this is the starting place for the phrase "hit the ceiling") changed its direction, dropped down, and swung like the first ringing of the Liberty Bell. Willie took

the whole medicine ball right in his face. He ducked
down and raised up again, this time taking the medicine ball in the back of his head.

"Willie, you look like you have lost a lot of weight.
How did you do it?" the barber asked.

"I lost thirty-one pounds. It took about thirty
days."

"Was it a special diet or something like that?"

"Not a special diet. I had all my teeth to come
loose and the dentist had to wire both of my jaws
shut. I could not eat anything solid. Mostly, I had
Gerber baby food mixed with water. I usually had
green beans, crushed bananas mixed with a little
beer. "

The men in the barber shop were amazed that
Willie came through such a thing. Willie was back.
Ball bats, bowling balls, worms, and turpentine
were all behind him. He had good tight teeth, two
strong jaws, and a knot on his forehead that most
doctors thought might go away in a couple of years.
Even the broken hall mirror that all said would be
seven years of bad luck no longer was something to
worry about. He had gone to Wallace McCall, one
of the best lawyers in the county, who told Willie
he could get him off for three or four years instead
of seven years.

C hristmas of 1957 gave Willie the opportunity to work part-time at the department store in Troy. Usually, Willie would work on the large grocers, sorting out canned beans and mopping the floors and pushing grocery carts back and forth to customers' car trunks. Farris Leach worked his way up the ladder and one more step would make him store manager. When Farris offered Willie the temporary shoe salesman, he jumped at the job. Willie was given a new suit of clothes, new shoes and a new smile.

Loretta Van Hoy was his third customer. She was just a little over three-hundred pounds and had feet larger than the average football player. The first two customers were the Kelly twins. Both girls wanted the first shoes they saw, their mother paid the clerk and they were gone in ten minutes. Loretta came in, wound her alarm clock and eased back on the white chair.

"Go get me a pillow, my back has been hurting. Hurry."

Willie disappeared for about ten minutes searching for a pillow. He finally found one on the third floor. He rushed back to Loretta.

"Where in the world did you go and why did you take so long?" Loretta berated Willie. "Go get all the shoes on the first aisle and I will start trying them on. This is going to take the rest of the day to get a good pair of shoes in this store."

Willie knew that the customer was always right, but Loretta was a little more than he could handle with only two days training. He smiled and went about his work of making sure Loretta got what she wanted and not what she deserved. Willie opened the first shoe box, placed his knees on the little white foot prop. He smiled with all of his charm, he slicked back his bald head and choosing a shoe, he bent forward. Loretta moved forward and pushed the pillow into place, she thought Willie's bald head was her knee.

So as graceful as possible she took her right hand and pulled her dress and petticoat over Willie's head. He nearly panicked with his head between her knees. Something told Loretta that she needed to move back. When she moved back the dress and petticoat fell and Willie's smiling face met her. She pushed hard on Willie and he slid backwards. "Pervert, pervert. Help me." In her terror she pushed the thirty-six box of Christmas cherry candy into the chair that held the candy. She ran out the door with candy running down her dress. Willie told those he worked with that he could not catch his breath for about an hour and he had to take his necktie.

It was not two hours later that the mother of all mothers strode in with a young boy. Children are the easiest to fit, he told himself. This was a polite young man and his mother.

"Hello, young man," Willie said.

"His name is Ja Van," his mother said with a blank face.

"Well, you just hop up into that chair and we will find the perfect shoe for you." Willie smiled.

"He wants to get brown shoes and about a size larger than his feet. That way if the teacher gives the class a dance, he could dye his shoes black and wear them to the gym."

"So you are a dancer?" Willie asked.

"No, he hates to dance and he would never dance with a girl. He can do the Montgomery Stomp but that ain't real dancing. He learned to dance from Loretta Van Hoy. She is his aunt."

"Poor little Ja Van. Is that your toe? That you toe? " His mother kept answering for him and she told him to take a pair of shoes and then they had to buy him some underclothes.

"I hope you come back some day," But, his mother might just run him crazy first. "I can just see little Ja Van and his mother trying on his underwear," Willie told Ray, his co-worker. "I can just hear her now. Is that------?"

The door opened and a smiling young man stepped in from the cold. He, too, wanted shoes. He had them picked out from watching them in the window. He dropped into the fitting chair, took his shoes off and leaned back. Willie was delighted. This customer was the best thing he had encountered all day. He kneeled and held a box of shoes to the smiling shopper. The young man ran his hand over Willie's bald head and laughed.

"What's so funny?" Willie said with a deeper voice.

"I just noticed, your bald head feels just like my wife's butt."

Willie hesitated for a minute, rubbed his bald head and laughed himself. "I have to agree with you, it feels like your wife's butt."

"Willie, you can be our Santa Claus. A little stuffing and you would look just like Santa Claus. I will be happy to switch you to the Christmas Gifts to children. If it was me, I would apologize for poking that customer in the nose. Just stay out of Loretta Van Hoy's way."

"Ho-ho-ho, and a Merry Christmas to all," Willie beamed like a star on to the cedar tree.

The three men met at Sally's Grill. It was on a beautiful Sunday morning. Like little kids sneaking off to get into some mischief, Willie and the two men were skipping church. None of the three was an expert at dodging the preacher and all three agreed to put a five dollar bill in the offering dish next Sunday. The good thing was that none of the three went to the same church. The day started off as usual with the men cooking breakfast and washing the breakfast dishes. All three played the "Honey, you don't look like you feel good. Maybe you ought to stay home and rest."

All three of their wives said the same thing. "I guess I do need a little rest. As soon as the wives lay back down their husbands left for church, the three men eased out and sneaked off. They had used that routine before, but not a lot. After three cups of coffee at Sally's, the next move was to go to the river. The water, the month, and the sun told them the fish were just waiting to be caught.

Waiting for the first bite, David said he felt a lot of shame, by all the lying and the hiding and he would not do this again. Leon said about the same thing. There was a lot of guilt in sneaking around and pretending to be sick. Willie said he was more ashamed than the other two. His wife was really sick and she could not get up that morning. He would check on her after he got home and cleaned the fish.

M iss Dooly was teaching the first grade. It was her first teaching job and she knew she would love it. Little Willie Jr. was also in the first grade. He had a habit of being restless and a little snoopy. Margret Hogan sat next to Willie Jr. and snitched on his every move.

"Miss Dooly, come see what Willie did."

From her experience, she hurried over to the window where Little Margret and Willie sat.

Margret pointed to a water spill between the two.

"Willie, is this water you spilled or is it something else?" Miss Dooly asked.

"Oh, it is tweat. It is hot over here, by the window. It is just tweat," Willie said.

Miss Dooly went back to her desk.

"Miss Dooly, come see what Willie done."

"Willie, what are you doing?"

"Miss Dooly, I told you that it is just tweat. I get hot and I tweat a lot."

Several minutes later the high voice of Margaret rang out again.

"Miss Dooly, Willie has his tweater out again."

While on an outing at the lake, Uncle Willie and several of the boys were on an overcrowded pontoon boat. As luck would have it, another boat bumped the pontoon boat, throwing several of the boys over the side into the deep water of the Pee Dee River.

A man came right up in another pontoon and as the men began to float to the surface, he would grab them by the hair of their head to drag them aboard his boat. When poor old bald headed Willie popped up, the man stared at him for a few minutes, then hit him on the top of his head with a boat paddle. "You go back down and come up right," he said.

The traffic on old highway 73 was slow and a back up on the road was slowing it down even more. About a mile from Wind Blow, the traffic was usually going fast, maybe faster than allowed. As the cars went passed, they blew their horns at Willie in anger.

A highway patrolman stopped and pointed for Willie to stop. "Why am I stopping you?"

"Because you can't catch them." Uncle Willie pointed to the line of cars.

L eon Temkin pointed up at the morning sun. "Look at that bird. What kind is it? It is big and blue."

"It might be the bird of paradise," Willie chuckled.

"Boy, he is a long way from home."

The lights of the carnival lit up the sky around the rides and the smoke from the diesel engines lay low on the ground covered with straw and pine naps. The smell of hot dogs, cotton candy, popcorn, and French fries mixed with the diesel engines and the flow of human sweat and body odor. This was the Fairway. All the games, all the geeks, all the places young boys wanted to go, went to the Fairway. Young children bobbed for plastic ducks with numbers printed on the underside that gave useless toys away. Men stood in the shooting gallery stand, firing off 22 bullets through a warped rifle barrel. But, the young teenage boys wanted just one peep at the Hoochie Gucci runway with over made up faces, women in their forties trying to shake whatever part of the body that turned someone on.

There were women in skimpy dresses twisting and pulling the mask to the side. Women who winked at the teenage boys and smiled. While standing at one of the runways, Willie Jr. was being hypnotized by one of these exotic dancers when Willie Sr. walked up. There was a stillness between the two. The father pointed to the rides.

"Boy, I want you to walk away. Do not go inside one of those places. If you do, you will see something you never want to see."

Like an embarrassed child, Willie Jr. took to his heels and dragged himself away. With only an hour left in the carnival, Grease Ball Hurley rounded the corner and there sat poor Willie Jr. with the look of destruction written on his face.

"What happened? Are you sick?"

"No. But I might as well be. Pop told me if I went into the dancers tent, I would see something I would not want to see."

"Tell me what you saw," Grease Ball hoped to hear something real bad.

"I saw my pop, sitting right up front on the first row."

Roger Robison hired Leroy Temkin and Willie to dig a septic tank, hook it up, and cover it up. Both men were tired after two days of shoveling, dragging, and there was very little to do and a few minutes to pick up their tools.

Across town there was a preacher that was finishing his sermon. One of the Johnson boys had stepped off a moving truck. He hardly knew all the Johnson boys, but the mother and father wanted him to preach the funeral so he promised he would. The preacher was just going out the door when his wife called him back. His Uncle Martin just had something like a heart attack. The family told him to come quickly and pray. He sat off for Sanford. The preacher tried to get someone to take over the funeral, but most of them were off drinking coffee in Pinehurst. Finally, one of the newest preachers answered his phone and agreed to pray over the coffin. The preacher rattled off a makeshift map and let the young preacher, just starting in the field of ministry, quickly read the directions.

He turned his twelve-year-old Ford to highway number 73. He wrote the little map too fast. Things began to get confused. There was a bend in the road, or was it another road. If it was another road then he needed to turn around and hunt a hill. There was something listed to pass the pond at the McCall farm. Time was passing and the young preacher was no closer to the funeral than he was.

Leroy Temkin and Willie were taking their fourth coffee break. They saw a lot of dust heading over the Old Morganton road. Whatever it was and where it was going, they could not figure it out. There were a few times that the old car would stop and then take off again. Time was no longer the problem. He would be late by an hour. Finally, Leroy and Willie finished their last break. The last few shovels full of dirt were scattered across the septic tank. The young minister saw the two men and the dirt. He stopped, ran toward the two men and opened his Bible, mumbled some words and then prayed for the mound of dirt. He ran back to his car and took off.

Leroy and Willie stood there. They could not believe that someone would pray over a septic tank. They just shook their heads and finished their work.

"I can't get over a preacher stopping and praying over a septic tank," Willie said.

"Well, this is your big day." Willie smiled toward Rose.

"I dreamed this lots of times. I always wanted to have a party on the lawn and have people to come. You have done miracles on the yard and the canvas tarp over the tables and food is perfect," Rose said.

"I've got to finish the parking places and that will not take long."

"I am so glad that Libby volunteered to help me with the cooking. She is a wonderful cook and we have very little left to do. I gathered all the mushrooms I found out behind the barn. Libby is going to make a gravy with them. Oh, this is so elegant."

"I worry about them toadstools you are cooking. Ain't some of them poison?"

"I have some books on mushrooms and I am sure they are the ones that can be cooked. I am taking a precaution. I am keeping a close watch on Spot and I have Libby keeping a sharp eye on him. If anything happens to that dog she will come straight to me.

I took some roast beef, mixed it with mushrooms, and I am keeping an eye on him. If you remember when I was in the garden club, we spent a whole month on studying nothing but mushrooms. Remember?"

"Remember? How could I forget? That was not a good thing. Eva Jane Miller was no doubt the first person to say she was poisoned. After that, it was one panic after another. All them getting their stomachs pumped out. I still call her Evil Jane."

"She will not be here today. One bit, twice learned."

Besides the eleven women, with Rose and Libby there would be eleven husbands. Men liked to smoke cigarettes and talk about farming and the preacher oddly enough was a storyteller. The sky was blue, no clouds to mess the feast up. Spot, the hungry dog was lying in a pile of lawn clippings. The fragrant smell of the coffee wafted in the air, all men sat with a cup in their hands.

At one o'clock, Willie used a large spoon and tapped on the bottom of a cast iron pot. The preacher shortened his blessing to about twenty minutes. The feast was on. Nothing could be better. All the food was gone by two and all the bellies were full. Libby stepped from the kitchen and motioned for Rose to come inside.

"Ma'am, you told me to keep an eye out for Spot. Spot is dead."

Rose froze for a good five minutes. Then she collected her wits and stepped to the telephone and began the ambulances and stomach pumps parade. Then she walked outside and destroyed everyone's day. Some chose to leave and get to the nearest hospital. Some decided to use the old throwing up method by two fingers pushed down their throats. The preacher dropped to his knees and begged forgiveness which really rattled his wife. Libby ran back out and had both hands on her hips. "I just cannot understand people like that."

"What do you mean?" Rose asked with trembling lips.

"They are just crude and inconsiderate. Ran over Spot and never stopped to let the owners know."

I was born in Virginia. After the Second World War ended, we moved to Biscoe, Montgomery County, North Carolina. There was something about Biscoe that enthralled me. It was my *Our Town*, Thornton Wilder and *Winesburg, Ohio*, Sherwood Anderson, a group of tales of Ohio. In 1965, the most beautiful woman in the world and I crossed the state line to get married and start a life together in Biscoe.

Dec. of 1965 my wife and I moved away.

I told stories at schools, churches, libraries, on front porches, social clubs, business meetings, guitar pickings and once for a Tennessee radio program. I wrote a popular newspaper column for *The Mooresville Tribune* for many years. My poetry won 8 NC state awards in as many years.

I always changed names to protect the guilty.

God sent us the hungry, the sad, the young with no family and those who needed to leave their family. Two children who lost their mother and father, good friends of ours.

And a young lady we called Nonie, who showed us how to love and a son Danny who put up with brothers and sisters he accepted as a family. He brought friends he thought needed help.

He was usually right.

60 years later, the most beautiful woman in the world, Dot, and I are still married. We have seen each other through thick and thin and when this adventure of life is over, we will see each other in the Here After.

Made in the USA
Columbia, SC
28 June 2024